The Greek Play

The Greek Play

Robert Manns

iUniverse, Inc.
Bloomington

The Greek Play

iUniverse books may be ordered through booksellers or by contacting:

iUniverse
1663 Liberty Drive
Bloomington, IN 47403
www.iuniverse.com
1-800-Authors (1-800-288-4677)

ISBN: 978-1-4401-4005-1 (sc)
ISBN: 978-1-4401-4004-4 (ebook)

Printed in the United States of America

iUniverse rev. date: 7/1/2011

Introduction

The Greek Play takes place about 218 B.C. when Rome, wanting a Spanish town of the Carthaginians, was refused the gambit by Hannibal, the Carthaginian military commander, and the Second Punic War began. Within a month, Hannibal was on his way to Rome with about 40,000 troops, including cavalry, light infantry and 37 battle elephants. But alighting from the Alps foothills, he possessed only 20,000 foot soldiers, 6,000 cavalry and one elephant. His subsequent victory over the 86,000-strong Roman army still lost him the war, but his invasion made history and was heard about around the Mediterranean, even into neighboring Athens.

Place

Epirus, Greece, perhaps a hundred miles northwest of Athens.

Cast

Tesup	A well-constructed man in his middle thirties
Antimodes	Older, say 45, an educated commoner
Proetus	A retired warrior of good carriage in his early sixties, on pension
Echo	The 80-year-old mother of Proetus
Dorthea	Attractive wife of Proetus, in her fifties
Aileen	An attractive woman in her mid-sixties
A Messenger	

Act One, Scene One

About 218 B.C. A small garden plot with a bench in front of Proetus' stone and thatch home. The home itself shows a main entry, a window each side of the door. Present are Tesup and Antimodes.

Act One, Scene Two

An interior room of Proetus' and Dorthea's home with tile floor, walls decorated with colorful frescoes. Tables and benches are plastered forms built onto, so attached to, the stone walls, which are also plastered. This room would serve as a modern living room. Present are Dorthea and Echo. Time: ten days later.

Act One, Scene Three

In the garden plot. Present are Proetus and a messenger. Time: several days later.

Act One, Scene Four

In the garden plot. Echo is dozing on the bench. Time: several weeks later.

Act One, Scene Five

In the garden plot. Antimodes is seated, waiting. Time: a week later.

Act Two, Scene One

In the garden plot. Echo is present, appliquéing. Time: three days later

Act Two, Scene Two

In the living room. Present are Proetus and Aileen. Time: a few minutes later.

Act Two, Scene Three

In a nearby wooded area. Present are Proetus and Aileen. Time: the following day.

Act Two, Scene Four

In the garden plot. Present are Proetus, Aileen and Dorthea. Time: next morning.

To Eileen Brewer nee Sochko

Act One

<table>
<tr><td>Scene One</td><td>In the garden plot. About 218 B.C. Present are Tesup and Antimodes.</td></tr>
</table>

Antimodes   A warm one is what I'd call this summer.

Tesup   Ah, warm it is, but still beats a cold one.

Antimodes   You think so?

Tesup   I know so, Antimodes.

Antimodes   Do you, really?

Tesup   Are you pulling my leg?

Antimodes   Not on a warm day; it would only stretch.
That would handicap you with Proetus.

Tesup   And on a cold one?

Antimodes   The poor leg would snap
and put you out of business with his need
of you entirely.

Tesup   Well, what's his need
then?

Antimodes	Can't you wait, Tesup?
Tesup	I suppose so but I think maybe you don't know at all.
Antimodes	Do you really think that of me, Tesup?
Tesup	I do; my leg is sore from it. Take it.
Antimodes	You will need it. I see him coming now.
Tesup	Well, I'd do anything for him, I guess. When we were neighbors, he treated me good.
Antimodes	Why did you move?
Tesup	Women here are taken. And he got the town prize, that Dorthea.

(Enter Proetus)

Proetus	Gentlemen, Antimodes and Tesup, friends of mine and my household, how are you?
Antimodes	Fine, and you, Proetus?
Tesup	Good, good.
Proetus	I'm well, Antimodes. I have tasks for you both, one I could only entrust to neighbors and those I know well.
Antimodes	Too well, Proetus, is how you've known us these last sev'ral years. And well enough is how we have known you, your favors and kind generosity.

Proetus	Tesup, you are up, are you, to travel? I don't think winged chariots are needed, but good horses will be. Great distances are involved.
Tesup	Lead on, Captain; I'm for it if new countries are involved. I am yours and yours alone to scour new areas for fresh ladies. Send me north, Proetus, where the breasts are smaller, the lips firmer, the legs longer, the trunk is an hourglass and the whole form is a full two meters more from the ground. I'm sick of these floozies that Zeus won't touch for good reason.
Proetus	Oh, well, the good stock is all taken, is that it?
Tesup	You know it is.
Proetus	Oh, with the certainty of Agamemnon, I do. You, Tesup, have a reputation.
Tesup	I don't favor a woman taken ever. Haven't, won't.
Proetus	So I hear. Now, Antimodes, you know the object of my quest here already— although the subject you have long forgot— it's the same lady I told you about some time ago that I'd experienced forty years ago as a young captain and could not erase from my memory
Antimodes	Oh, I remember that confidence now.

Proetus	Well, I remember it daily and more. And a goodly marriage of many moons won't erase her memory. Confound it, she was a beauty of both mind and frame. She knew all the secrets of the Far East and Alexandria, housed massive love in all the heart's compartments, believe me, and exercised that love with due passion, Antimodes.

(To Tesup)

Antimodes	And just forty years gone; a captain's tribute to the fair, fair sex, Tesup.

Tesup	I hear, but she won't be fair now. If she's dead, she'll be ages old in 'er grave and if she's living still, out of the grave, by all the gods, she'll be out of passion, also. So what are we looking for, then?

Proetus	A relevant question, Tesup. Listen, we will research whatever is left there. Should she be dead, we will find her records. She was married and I know about where. I think, too, she was well provided for. Also, I know the climate she welcomed since I met her in it.

Antimodes	Did she survive her husband?

Proetus	I dreamt that she had done that.

Antimodes	And you trust—?

Proetus   I would thank one of the gods
                    if he exists and still gives her comfort.
                    I don't know which one.

Antimodes   Then what?

Proetus   I am a good man; I would wait my turn.

Tesup   What if, as probable, we find nothing,
                    no one?

Proetus   Then if the cost is not too dear,
                    I accept my fate. If it is too dear,
                    I accept the double loss. "Woe is me"
                    is not in my lexicon of feelings.
                    (Proffering a map…)
                    Here, Antimodes, is a crude drawing
                    of your first area of search, a place
                    where his business would have thrived, indeed,
                    profited, and the weather would please her.
                    (…and a purse)
                    And your advance; I ask for wisdom here.

Antimodes   As ever, Proetus.

Proetus   (Another map…)
                                    And you, Tesup,
                    up to Macedonia with you, then
                    southern Dacia. I can't guarantee
                    a full two meters in height for your lass,
                    but you might get sev'ral centimeters.

Tesup   Macedonia is good, Dacia
                    even better, being more northerly.
                    I hear the mountain women in both wear
                    you out, though, if well fed. So I can't wait.

Proetus	(…and a purse) If I didn't know you better, Tesup, I would tell myself I financed your trip to an exploration of your pleasures, not to any of mine.
Tesup	I am glad you know me, Proetus.
Proetus	I am deep down into my captaincy funds if our game goes to innings, so try to make this do, my friends.
Tesup	My friend, I thought this down payment on a vaster sum. I was figuring to make enough to hire help this winter in my fields.
Proetus	Well, I hope you will starve, then.
Tesup	Very unkind, my friend.
Proetus	Very adroit, too.
Tesup	I'll make do.
Antimodes	For my part, I've this to say: I humbly thank you for my employment, and may the gods be as gracious to you.
Proetus:	Thank you, Antimodes.
Tesup	I thank you too, Antimodes.

Proetus	Have either of you heard the news from Rome?
	It staggers a man's imagination.
	War conducted by a youth, Hannibal,
	the Carthaginian, who would avenge
	his father, Hamilcar Barca, who lost
	both his last battle and life to great Rome…
	This son is mustering large armed forces
	in Gaul and, it's rumored, some elephants
	to transport their supplies for the warfare
	into the north of the boot and to Rome.
	Carthage will lose it all, I should think.
Antimodes	Well,
	I should think so, too, Rome has vast forces.
Tesup	Winner take all, I say; just cut me loose
	for Macedonia, and then that Dacia.
Proetus	One more word, then, and I will let you go.
	The woman's name, Aileen, is on your maps
	with some small description from memory
	and her married name. Remember always
	that she was and is of primal brilliance
	to the African diamond and still more
	gold than citrine. Imagine that, will you.
	And although jade was her best color then,
	the emerald will sing to her now, I think.
	Oh, tourmaline, perhaps, not peridot.
	But confront her and then make her angry,
	and you will set atremble a black opal,
	ruby spinel and bloodstone in one brooch.
	However, emotive as I knew her,
	she never once voiced anger in our time.
	Count on the light and livid chrysoprase
	for her demeanor should you chance on her.
	Remember, she is the peach of my mind's
	eye, a conjuration the sun's own rays

or moon's white light could not eradicate.
I love my wife; she is nearest me, and
I intend to keep her nearest to me.
I court Aileen as valued memory.
Go find her, I beg you.

Antimodes   He's stuffed with her.

Tesup   A stuffed shirt, eh?

Antimodes   You might say so, Tesup.

Tesup   You notice? I just did.

Proetus   Have fun with me.
                 Keep the game brief, but do clear it to win.

Tesup   I'm off, Antimodes, with goats to milk
                 and to Macedonia.

Antimodes   I see here
                 that he sends me south, by Hecuba, south.
                 To Athens, laddie. I've never been there.

Tesup   Well, bring me back news of it.

Antimodes   Yes, I will.

(Enter Echo)

Antimodes   Dear Echo, I will tell you once again
                 you have a most adventurous fellow
                 for a son but, of sons, one of the best,
                 one with the most enduring fortitude.
                 Good day to you.

Tesup   Good day, Madam Echo.

Echo	The day's greetings to both you gentlemen.

(Exit Antimodes and Tesup)

Proetus	Oh, Echo—dear Mother, more appliqué? Do you apply it to placate a god? If so, which one? You know we have enough of those to go around. Well now, Cadmus, after learning those deadly secrets taught to Iasion by Zeus married then to Harmonia, child of one Ares and Aphrodite. It was the first known mortal wedding attended by the gods. Then Demeter assured Harmonia a good barley harvest by lying with Iasion in a thrice ploughed grassland. Mother, do you wish to believe them gods or manmade deities, manmade altars in a manmade edifice? Oh, by Zeus!
Echo	Care, care, Son. You'll waken the big fellow and bring down the fate of Prometheus on us all.
Proetus	But that courageous thinker gave us his life.
Echo	He certainly did that.
Proetus	And gave us power Zeus had lost to him: the power of freedom of thought.
Echo	Nonsense.
Proetus	You think so?

Echo   I do.

Proetus   Then I'm stalled again.

Echo   He lost it, you know.

Proetus   Wagon stuck in mud.

Echo   You'll lose that wagon someday, someday soon.
               Your dazed arguments for Prometheus
               are almost ripe enough now to forsake
               the branch that nursed them. How you do babble.

Proetus   Well, I have something more urgent for you,
               then, touching down on the heart as you like.
               Woe, setting the heart on such a quick pace
               that its drumming shakes the delicate frame
               it stands in. Here it is: I am in love.

Echo   Hang your head; you have a wife.

Proetus   Yes, I know,
               and one I love, one I did contract to.
               Dorthea, I love; she is my partner
               in life and will remain until that life
               in one body fails to waken, Mother.
               But years ago, some forty, I knew one
               woman who made the world spin at breakneck
               speeds. We were lovers for four golden years,
               sharing a small house, no acrimony,
               no cross-purposes, nothing undisclosed
               almost, a simple Olympian life.
               Then one day, she was offered employment
               far away when my poor fortunes had ebbed,
               and I let her go. Toss of the damned dice.

Echo   Well, a story of broken hearts, is this?

Proetus	For forty years, I had casual thoughts and even dreams of her, and then was one, supposing she had married, of her loss of a good and responsible husband.
Echo	That was Aileen, I take it.
Proetus	Well taken, Mother.
Echo	We were apart so many years but I remember your speaking of her. But so what? She could have joined her husband by this time.
Proetus	I want to discover that for myself. And if she is with us still, I want her here.
Echo	Oh, madness, Proetus! Dorthea would be stricken! She would die a thousand deaths. No, she has a temper; someone else might—
Proetus	No, I'd reveal to her the whole story, when it happened and how and give her assurances of my love till she was ill of them and called me off. She will understand me, on my honor.
Echo	All this time, Proetus, and still you don't understand women. Find her if you must, love her if you must, but do not bring her here. Men fight whole wars for territories large as cities, states and entire nations, continents even. Women strike for homes.

Proetus	Not to live, Mother, merely to visit.
Echo	Out of the question, Son.
Proetus	To my own home, run by my officer's retirement?
Echo	Good officers must often have listened to their superiors for some advice, no?
Proetus	Yes, I did sometimes, I suppose.
Echo	Well, I have never been your superior before.
Proetus	You may never be again, too. The idea of my own home being closed to love is desert behavior to me. Nor will I have it be; you trust to that, Mother. This case will be an open file, a public knowing of it invited, welcome and even advertised by word. The transcendent aspect of love is law and will be obeyed on this property. I hope you hear.
Echo	So I do, Proetus.

Scene Two.	**In the living room. Present are Dorthea and Echo. Time: ten days later.**

Echo

Well, I am happy he still favors you,
Dorthea, because if my son were mad
enough to think other thoughts than your own
I don't know what I would do. Talk to him
would stuff his ears.

Dorthea

                              No, when he first told me
of her, and the number of times he dreamt
and thought of her, I must confess I cried.
But then he, so touched and so tenderly,
convinced me of his love that he tamed me
completely, washing away faulty fears
and those all too foolish speculations
one makes without a dram of reasoning.
I do confess to seeing a raven
in the east sky hearing of her wisdom,
her beauty and her ardent homemaking,
but again, he spoke of mine as finest.
It is a poor day when a simple wife
can't even trust a forty-year-old dream
in her man. He has been forthright with me,
Echo.

Echo

        It's important that you think so,
my dear, since envy born of doubt and fear
belonged to so many of our own gods
that we may take warning there.

Dorthea

                                        Echo, thanks.

Echo

What news from Antimodes and Tesup,
have you heard?

Dorthea	They've just been gone some ten days.
Echo	Twenty, more like. My time is all night time till I hear.
Dorthea	What do you expect to hear?
Echo	That she is dead, I think. Dreams are dead end.
Dorthea	Then I hope not, for his sake.
Echo	Oh, Hermes, only simple women are permissive.
Dorthea	But why would I wish to hurt Proetus?
Echo	Better to hurt him than all of us, no? You know he wants to bring her here, you fool.
Dorthea	Here? Nothing of here, I'm told. Bring her here?
Echo	Ah!
Dorthea	Why?
Echo	So that you may see he's honest as a shepherd charged with a valued flock. That's why! Why, he wants you to welcome her.
Dorthea	She cannot come here. She must not.
Echo	Tell him!
Dorthea	No, it is his house, but if she does come, she will earn this. (She picks up a small urn from a table)

Echo	No, my girl, that could wound.
Dorthea	Just the thing, to send her home with a wound.
Echo	She might report you to authorities; then where would we be? In the tribune's courts.
Dorthea	She report me?! She comes to my home hunting my husband, and I should worry that I may hurt her. Pah, Echo, shame, shame! I'll make a cudgel of an oak tree limb and that will put a dent in her, I swear.
Echo	What if she takes it from you, my dear girl, and assaults you with it? We know nothing of the woman's size or inclinations.
Dorthea	Assault me, would she? Then something more sure is in order, and I would offer her my home's finest and sharpest certainty: a well-honed blade! (She unsheathes a knife from a table)
Echo	Oh, the gods help us now.
Dorthea	You note no gods disturb our wars, Echo, why think they have concern for one meat knife? If she is a bitch, a dog's death to her! She will not wrap her legs around my man or even so much as warp his bedding! Ay! Even so much as enter this house! Ay! We do what we must!
Echo	I hope her dead.

Dorthea	Everything in this house marked Proetus
	is his, all things marked Proetus are mine
	since I belong to Proetus and you,
	Echo, to us because we love you. That
	ownership is ours and will be kept ours.
	(She re-sheathes the knife)
	He may respect her at a great distance
	but not within these walls or properties.

Dorthea Everything in this house marked Proetus
is his, all things marked Proetus are mine
since I belong to Proetus and you,
Echo, to us because we love you. That
ownership is ours and will be kept ours.
(She re-sheathes the knife)
He may respect her at a great distance
but not within these walls or properties.

Echo I knew you had the temper to defeat
a legion of shields, but not violence,
Dorthea. That is no good in this house.

Dorthea No good in any house or anywhere,
but does settle things.

Echo   Not for the best, though.

(Enter Proetus)

How are things in the orchard, Son?

Proetus   Ah, fine.
Mother, we'll have a good crop of olives.
The mothering trees that have nurtured them
captured a resisting earth, clement air
and our generous sun again this year.
You will have kalamatas in your dreams.

Echo Don't want them in my dreams, just on my plate
with their leaves or sea grapes or anything.
Oil and serve, I say.

Proetus   Good market crop, too.
Why, what's the matter here?

Echo   Between us two?

Proetus	Anyone or with anything.
Dorthea	Echo?
Proetus	Yes, or with Echo.
Echo	I think she asked me if I were meant or something close to that, Proetus.
Proetus	Are you both in touch with Greek today?
Echo	What do you mean, Son?
Proetus	My meaning? What is yours?
Echo	I'm confused, confused, my son.
Proetus	More than one of us is shielding something. I hear we have a word for everything; take advantage of your wealth.
Dorthea	Proetus, we were talking women's talk, but nothing. In Echo's defense, that is our problem: revealing unloaded, unint'resting gossip to your ever-inquiring mind.
Proetus	Now, now, I think it had to do more with the newest subject sprung amongst we three.
Dorthea	That is—?
Proetus	The latest play of Sophocles.

Dorthea   You play, my love, you play.

Proetus   Indeed, I do.

Echo   What is the sense of all this, Proetus?

Proetus   Two against one, Mother?

Echo   Yes, but I quit.

Proetus   So now, Dorthea.

Dorthea   It was; it was, then,
               about your lady and your sending out
               Tesup and Antimodes to find her,
               which is not likely, to my simple mind.

Proetus   But why deny it?

Echo   Why not? It's hardly
               our favorite subject.

Proetus   Oh, but why not?

Echo   It is yours who wouldn't want it usurped,
               I think.

Proetus   Take, run and throw that javelin,
               ladies, it belongs to those who launch it.
               Make it sing in the air. Oh, make it sing
               till melody itself lies embarrassed.

Echo   He wants to know what we will not tell him,
               Dorthea.

Dorthea   Then let's tell him.

Echo	All?
Dorthea	Yes, all.
Echo	A small falcon flew in the window blind after a pipit who made it safely, but the falcon torn a wing nearly off, and we buried it near the west vineyard.
Proetus	I had asked you to identify birds or to call me. What of that?
Dorthea	Well, of that we knew, but the falcon succumbed to shock and died, so we felt best to bury him.
Proetus	Just careless, both of you. Whether it was a hobby, kestrel or lanner falcon no one will know since you played caretaker. Well now, if you will—next time, ladies, please.
Echo	We will, Proetus.
Proetus	Next time, if you will do measure him, at least.
Echo	Oh, yes, we will.
Proetus	More news of Hannibal, that Carthage rat, who, it seems, will plague Rome now to time's end. He has swelled his ranks with some say fifty elephants, and he thinks to make the Alps his roadway into the alpine regions, there to enlist new troops for his mainland thrust. But he is a youthful general who depends too much on colorful war.

His elephants, never groomed for mountains.
will suffer again human ignorance,
slowing his progress, providing targets
of a size unknown to human warfare.
Still, his battles, like all war, will cost Rome.

Echo   I wish he had come across our waters.

Proetus   He would have been destroyed by our navy.

Echo   That's why I wished it.

Proetus   I doubt he'll profit.

(A knock at the door)

(Enter Tesup)

Tesup   May I enter?

Proetus   By all means, do, Tesup.
Not gone a fortnight and you have good news?

Tesup   Speak freely?

Proetus   Speak as freely as birds fly
and bear me good news as our swallows do.
The ladies are apprised of all our work
toward finding Aileen. Give us news, Tesup,
to brighten the day.

Tesup   Well, I think it's news,
all right, but to brighten the day, I doubt
it has that strength.

Proetus   I will take whatever.

Tesup	It surprised me totally. I landed on the other side of Lilanth River just out of Amphipolis, and behold! I met a man who seemed to know Aileen, not by her married name, though, another that was foreign to me. But I tracked her to her house, and she promptly assured me she was the one you sought.
Proetus	Well, so then what?
Tesup	I thought she was lying.
Proetus	How so, lying?
Tesup	Well, no woman, to my mind, wants to be claimed by one man when she is in her bed with another one. She was that, all right; I could see the man past her in his skin and no more, and so I leave it to you whether she fits the bill or not. I see her looking something like what you gave me, with the added near half a century, of course. She is now far from a looker, but I have a feeling in my gut here, despite the lie, she may be the woman.
Proetus	Here in my gut, I feel that your judgment has capsized in very shallow water, even before battle, with gun ports closed. The woman I seek would not belittle my cause or efforts. She might dismiss me but not my purpose, which is all public and noble. I have published it in town. You struck a reef, Tesup, in some shallows, and should make more inquiry as you go. You must search the face of your answerer,

his body movements, hers. Next find a clue
that leads to truth or falsehood, then move on
if the truth leads nowhere worthy of you.

Tesup   I will, good sir.

Proetus   You made a blazing start
that will teach you caution and discretion
and, in those observations, a new mode
or process of manner designed for thought.

Tesup   Something to think about, Proetus.

Proetus   Yes.

Tesup   Ladies: Dorthea, Echo

(Exit Tesup)

Proetus   A good young man. Too many ambitions
of a lowly order. He is too pleased
with his composition to know the worth
of it. His broad shoulders are for women's
eyes only, his small waist the exact same.
Mother, I need a word with Dorthea,
if you please.

Echo   I will tend the new herb patch.

(Exit Echo)

Dorthea   Are you angry?

Proetus   With what, my love?

Dorthea   With me.

Proetus   I have no intent of anger with you.

Dorthea   None? About the falcon?

Proetus   Never a bird,
Dorthea.

Dorthea   Then about my fervent wish
to dwarf the name and image in this house
of your Aileen or whatever her name
till something erases her from our lives.
I cannot, will not, share a good husband
with any woman, new or old, on earth.

Proetus   No such need, Dorthea.

Dorthea   I think you lie.

Proetus   Dorthea!

Dorthea   You told me she was miles off.

Proetus   For all I know, she is. I don't know where
she is. It could be Germania, worse,
England, Lapland, who knows where?

Dorthea   I doubt you.

Proetus   Then let me repeat all I have told you.
The quest for Aileen is a quest for truth
and beauty.

Dorthea   There! You say all the wrong things.

Proetus   Both of those are found in statuary;
both of those, too, are found in colonnades,
in tiled figurines, in textiled figures.

Dorthea	Art is a lie.
Proetus	Oh, granted; it's that, too. If it does not more than describe itself, it is a copy of the thing described, nothing added, naught withdrawn, featureless and aimless, nothing ventured, nothing gained. A lie, but still more than duplication, Dorthea. But we were on a lady here, not art, for surely she is not art but more.
Dorthea	More wrong things! You are full of them!
Proetus	I must try harder, keep my sandals from off Olympus but foot out of my mouth. Do forgive my little anxieties about big subjects. They uproot forests of good intentions and supplant the whole with brushy acreage of lesser means. I have been open with you to a fault, perhaps, but open with you I will be. Dorthea, I have given legal word to you that I, to you, am wed for life. No similar word was spent on Aileen. Nor will word be. Ours was a diff'rent time of diff'rent needs. We spent those four prime years in a kind of solitude still unknown to man; we two walked the plank to heaven. Then she found employment elsewhere and I, not knowing good reason to prevent her, threw up my arms to the necessary. Well, she married and division was pat. As I've told you, it was ethereal, of another world, not Greek or Roman. I want love and respect paid to her now if she remains, and will expect the same from all within this house, by Hecuba.

Dorthea	Zeus, you rarely swear by gods.
Proetus	True, rarely.
Dorthea	Well, I will swear by mine to face her with honesty is all, and hope that candor is all that needs be.
Proetus	My thanks, Dorthea.
Dorthea	I will be just as honest with you, too. A visit, even, from such a woman who cares so little for my position bears witness, does it not, to a trollop? There are few women who would do what she would do.
Proetus	I don't know the answer to that. But we are far, far ahead of ourselves. Is she alive? Would she be int'rested in me as I am in her? We don't know. She may have felt her years with me jail time and too slow over. She was a jewel in a rough setting.
Dorthea	Oh, and still one more!
Proetus	I see that winning this one is a loss in the making and will leave you to it.
Dorthea	Ay! Leave me to it! Forget your poor wife and leave her to her putrid wretchedness! Give her twenty years of matrimony, a kiss and walking papers. Come on, now. If ever you looked for liberation, it looks at you with eager eyes.

Proetus	The Spites,
	out of their jar, spill over Scylla's form,
	and something so bountiful is made mean.
	War between man and wife is best treated
	quickly or not at all.

Dorthea	Kiss me, Husband.

Proetus	It would be a hollow trumpet, woman.

(Exit Proetus)

Dorthea	Ay! And the kiss would mean nothing to you,
	too aged and dry to implement much more.

(Enter Echo)

Echo	Dorthea, I heard, the field hands heard you.
	What happened?

Dorthea	Nothing, and that's the problem.

Echo	You have made everyone aware of you;
	they whisper you have suddenly gone mad.

Dorthea	He left saying she does not exist yet
	and that I'm too early with objection.
	Imagine that!

Echo	Well, there is some sense there.
	Proetus can be sensible at times—

Dorthea	Oh, no, now you side with him! You're fickle.

Echo	Sensible at times if you let him be.

Dorthea   Oh, Echo, have I been unfair with him?
Please tell me; I do so trust you.

Echo   Well, yes.
It is true, as he says, that voids matter
not, and we both may have gone off the deep
end before we had patiently heard him
out. Women make a habit of quickness,
too, you know, but more often with less truth,
Dorthea.

Dorthea   Have I been a fool?

Echo   Fool? Mouse?
Woman concerned for the loss of her man?
All of those. We both jumped the starter's gate
and ran a mythical race to nonsense.

Dorthea   Oh, I will be sick.

Echo   My son will forgive.
He has learned that well from his blessed father
before that good man died. I may have drummed
it home a few times, too. But he forgives.

Dorthea   I went to see a marionette show
last year, in which one character faded
into the set and vanished. I wish I
could do likewise.

Echo   He won't have you do that,
on my word.

Dorthea   I heard a bell.

Echo   When?

Dorthea   Just now;
            listen.

Echo   My old ears hear nothing these days.

Dorthea   There, again. Closer.

Echo   That's a messenger
            bell, and we must hope not for Proetus.

Scene Three. **In the garden plot. Present are Proetus and a messenger. Time: several moments later.**

Messenger   Antimodes says it may be false luck,
but she answers to the name of her spouse,
her married name and that of their bus'ness.

Proetus   As the hawk said of the nest of rabbits,
"Yum, yum," sir. That is a healthy report.
How does she look?

Messenger   No description, Captain.
He says she is time worn.

Proetus   And that's all, sir?

Messenger   Yes. He told me she was once good looking
but that all the gods had declared her done.
Does that afflict you?

Proetus   No, sir, no pain there;
at her age and mine, I am not running
a beauty contest. Oh, Antimodes
has sent me a puzzle and a caution.

Messenger   He notes that she has eaten well and taken
care of herself more or less, if that counts
in her favor. May I ask a question?

Proetus   Well, I had hoped I would ask the questions,
but ask away.

Messenger   It's a difficult one,
Captain.

Proetus   You overcame the difficult
distance from Athens.

Messenger	Indeed, yes, Captain.
Proetus	That qualifies you.
Messenger	Are you buying her, Captain?
Proetus	I had no idea of that, sir.
Messenger	Antimodes says she wishes to know how much you will put on her; she means gold.
Proetus	By the gods, and I mean all of them, sir, unless the lady I seek has fallen on hard times—and that is most unlikely since her husband would have left her content— I would in person come to her post-haste. But to "put" gold on an unknown product is to speculate far beyond my means.
Messenger	So no gold?
Proetus	So no gold. And no copper, even, or sympathy either if she is the lady I seek, since she has killed the image of the one I much desired. Then I'm left with a conscience for the step I take. What if she is, indeed, Aileen? What a scoundrel I am to turn her down in this an hour of need. What would you do?
Messenger	I'd tell her to go to Hades, good sir.
Proetus	Even in the face of the possible?

Messenger	Oh, yes, even the probable, I would. Think about it. Takes gold from a stranger, next takes it from a friend, then from a corpse. Who can trust such a wench? Not me, not you, if you give it some thought. That's what I'd do, anyway. Women begging gold, good sir, belong where they are—with two outstretched arms.
Proetus	You make a hard case.
Messenger	I do a tough job. You try it sometime, walking your legs off, getting a cart ride or a horse, maybe, fording streams, but mainly walking your legs and butt off. Well, you just try it sometime.
Proetus	I will confess I lack the proper years for it. So, perhaps in another life.
Messenger	You lucky gentry that have more than one.
Proetus	Wouldn't we be, though. Sir, before you leave, go into the house where my wife has made some cakes and poured you some wine to move you back to Antimodes in some comfort.
Messenger	Much obliged, good sir. What for the lady in Athens?
Proetus	Take some wine for her, too. Tell her to drink deep.
Messenger	I will.

(Exit the messenger into the house)

Proetus	(Thinking aloud) I never thought that finding her would be easy or even possible maybe, but I never thought to find a quagmire of Grecian witches either, I must say.

(Enter Echo)

Echo	Son, the squash beds are thriving, due to you.
Proetus	Well, no, they have had good care.
Echo	Yes, that too, but your suggestions last year that the beds be given more room has worked some wonders; there is little spoilage.
Proetus	Well, there is some.
Echo	Dorthea is still angry.
Proetus	She will be until not. There is nothing I can do to cure anger after pleading pain, sense, a broader wisdom. Dorthea will cure in her time. Sooner is always better, but it will be her time. People order time that way. Anger is more demanding than ration, taking more concentration from the angry and the poor listener.
Echo	Oh, tush.
Proetus	I promise it is tough on both of them, Mother.
Echo	Tush, tush on that, too, I suppose.

32

Proetus   Well, have you heard of the elephant's tush
and the fly that was on it?

Echo   What nonsense!

Proetus   But have you?

Echo   Of course not.

Proetus   I figured not.

Echo   Dorthea requires closer attention,
Proetus, you should see to it, my son.

Proetus   Well, then, the fly on the elephant's tush.

Echo   What elephant?

Proetus   One of Hannibal's own,
in fact. The fly, a long-life African
fellow that attached to Jumbo's hind end
and, try to believe it—

Echo   Proetus, stop!

Proetus   He had in mind—

Echo   Son, don't you understand—?

Proetus   He had—

Echo   Stop it. I don't care what he had!
This has taken on so many shadows
I'm at a loss for finding some daylight!

Proetus   This elephant—

Echo	I give up, I give up. Is that what you want?
Proetus	Exactly, Mother. (Two, three beats)
Echo	Then what is it about this elephant?!
Proetus	I've forgotten.
Echo	Then go see your dear wife.
Proetus	No need; here she comes. She has fed the boy.

(Enter Dorthea)

Dorthea	That lad was hungry, Proetus, hungry, but took only water in his wineskin. He says fools drink wine or beer when they work. A conscientious fellow, by my book.
Proetus	Who carried no good news for Proetus.
Dorthea	It was of Olympian size to me; I begged him come again with something like and I would bake him twice the count of cakes.
Proetus	He ate well?
Dorthea	And drank deep all the water he could hold till he got to the wood edge, where I'm sure he made a sizeable swamp.
Proetus	I'm sure Mercury's winged feet got him there.
Dorthea	He was a nice boy, he, brusque but civil.

Proetus	And he brought the news you were pleased to hear.
Dorthea	Oh, that he did.
Proetus	Did our good messenger relate the lady's wish to you, my love?
Dorthea	She wanted money, I think.
Proetus	Gold, no less.
Dorthea	That's a clever one!
Proetus	I dread it was she, however.
Dorthea	If it was, she burned her cards. And good for her if she did. Then she died saving us various ills of the heart and me a husband in the bargain.
Proetus	Unnecessary and cruel, Dorthea, and as much like you as new facial hair.
Dorthea	Well, would you like to see me grow a beard, my errant husband, or grow sun blisters on my skull top from a merciless sun? Which disfigurement would you favor me with, my wandering and cold Proetus?
Proetus	Oh, Dorthea!
Echo	This is all quite useless, as Proetus says, Dorthea.
Dorthea	Useless?!

Echo	If she has burned her cards, it is useless.
	She is out of the game and can go home.
	Then she died, as you say, saving us ills.
	To moan a mere viable and insult
	its conveyor seems an imbroglio
	of the first order against my good son.
	Proetus loves you; I have his promise,
	and what he promises exists. Trust me,
	too, to have that right. Or deny me it
	and him his and consume the world with hate.
	I think you may have walked too far today.
Dorthea	What? I have been in the kitchen all day.
Echo	That's it! A need for exercise, I swear!
	You have been kitchened too long.
Proetus	Dorthea,
	we will go together and smell the earth.
	We will go together in the orchard,
	in the far fields where we have new-mown hay,
	to the hedges where the rock buntings breed
	and sing their joy and back to the old fields
	for the wheatear's song and the path return
	along banks of blood hibiscus. Will you?
Dorthea	I would be a fool not to, Proetus.
Proetus	Take my hand.
Dorthea	I will.
Proetus	My hand taking yours
	is sign of the bull caressing his calf,
	sign of Indian tiger caressing
	her cub and eagle, her eaglet.

Dorthea	Thank you,
	my husband. A woman's assurances
	can never be numbered enough, I think.
Proetus	This raft has weathered both wars and rough seas,
	and here we surprisingly are in love
	and the majesty of one's twosomeness.
Dorthea	Will we weather more, d'you think?
Proetus	Well, do you?
Dorthea	Oh, I don't know, Proetus.
Proetus	Well, I do.
Dorthea	Then tell me. I am the dog in this fight
	carrying my tail low down between back legs,
	my ears down and eyes lower. I am whipped
	by it. So tell me.
Proetus	It will all vanish,
	I'm afraid.
Dorthea	And I'm afraid it will not.
	Let us go and smell the earth, then. Lead on.

Scene Four.   **In the garden plot. Echo is dozing on the bench.**
Time: several weeks later. After a number of beats—

(Enter Antimodes)

Antimodes   (After some discomfort, not knowing how to proceed)
Come, Echo, the day is passing—
(when there is no response)
                                                                    you by.
It's a long way from Athens, I tell you.
Carrying news like I do is heavy
work and does add to a body's labor.
(when there is no response)
Oh, say, you must have heard me. I know you
as closely as your goats do, your coming
and going. But I know what will rouse you,
Echo!!

Echo   I hear you, Antimodes. Oh,
yes, I heard you say the day is passing.
You put on my years, and you'll wake slowly
enough, too.

Antimodes   Fancy! You could hear me speak,
but not moving a sinew, hardly spoke.

Echo   It's a time-delay we elderlies have
to confuse the likes of you messengers.

Antimodes   Well, no confusion here.

Echo   Oh, you say so.

Antimodes   Is Proetus in?

Echo   Is your woman found?

39

| Antimodes | That goes to Proetus. |

| Echo | I'm his mother,
You dolt! |

| Antimodes | (Laughing)
You don't help him on with his underclothes
Still, do you? |

| Echo | He's inside, then. Proetus!! |

(Enter Proetus to the door, then proceeding)

| Proetus | Ah, my dear Antimodes! |

| Antimodes | Yes, Captain,
with apologies for my messenger.
Am I to give the news to you both here? |

| Proetus | If it is good news, do give it to me.
If it is bad, give it to my mother;
she will regale in it. |

| Antimodes | I do choose you,
my friend. |

| Echo | Oh, Achilles will do his dirt
on Hector after all, but let Hector
not be my Proetus. No, not my son. |

(Exit Echo)

| Antimodes | If you meant not to give it her, we failed,
Proetus. |

Proetus	No matter. She would commune with her gods whatever your fit answer. She keeps regular company with them.

Antimodes   And I, too, for some convincing signal
that your Aileen still took the Grecian air.
She does, my friend, and it much becomes her.
Shocked she was, no stupefied, by your call
for her through me. She froze with disbelief
and counted on her fingers forty years.
All this after answering to her names,
first marriage, second and her maiden name
even. She was living with relatives
by her second marriage, and had been left
carefree by him. She is nobility
on the hoof, Proetus. You have found her.

Proetus   I am staggered. Please let me sit a while.

Antimodes   Had you no training as a good captain
you would have been freed of your chariot
and sent sprawling to the ground with delight.

Proetus   How does she look now?

Antimodes   A few years older
than you, with the mentality of youth.
She smiles well, but Dorthea does that, too.

Proetus   Please, friend, only her differences for now.
How does her height compare to mine?

Antimodes   Like mine,
no more.

Proetus   And her weight?

Antimodes	Compared to what, please?
Proetus	Why, a horse.
Antimodes	Much lighter.
Proetus	A healthy doe?
Antimodes	Probably, and looking for a fine buck.
Proetus	None of that matters. We have found her, yes?
Antimodes	Count on it.
Proetus	Oh, I am, I am, my friend. My plentiful doubts are washed well away. Is she happy? Did you find her content?
Antimodes	She seemed comfortable.
Proetus	Did she seem happy hearing you out about my fervent search both to the north and south?
Antimodes	Delirious, not just happy.
Proetus	You are mocking me now.
Antimodes	No, sir, the pay is not enough to mock.
Proetus	And lippy, too. Now, if you were no Greek and not loved by me, I'd pay no bonus to you at all for your outstanding find. But you are all of those: lippy, Grecian, and loved by all, and I will send you some tomorrow.

Antimodes   By Hermes, that's far too much,
            Proetus.

Proetus   No bonus is too much, sir.
            Do go back and ask if I may visit
            at the address you give me, as you will,
            and when to expect me at her leisure.
            For now, go home and rest and tomorrow
            grow wealthy. You have done a potent piece.

Antimodes   There is no need for a second journey.
            Proetus. Here is her Athens address.
            She says, "Come soon and thus make forty years
            be felled like an oak," and I say, "No drachms."

Proetus   Antimodes, you have passed all my hopes
            in this venture and leave me quite standing
            in a pool of wonder, cool to the feet.
            You will keep the money I send, by god,
            or—

Antimodes   Swearing by god from a godless man!

Proetus   Taught gods when a child is hard to turn back,
            sir. Leave the language to my happiness.
            I will leave yours to you.

Antimodes   Thanks, Proetus.

(Exit Antimodes)

Proetus   (Calling)
            Dorthea! Dorthea!

Dorthea   (In the doorway)
                        Yes.

43

Proetus	Come here, please

(Enter Dorthea)

Proetus	I will go to the village tomorrow with the fawn horse to rent a chariot and proceed to our capital, Athens. I will need clean tunics for several days and personals. Please see to it, will you?
Dorthea	To Athens. Why to Athens, Proetus? Did Antimodes find your lost maiden there? I think he was to scout Athens, no?
Proetus	Was to and did.
Dorthea	Ay, then she was found there.
Proetus	Yes.
Dorthea	And I'm to be left alone, I think.
Proetus	Yes.
Dorthea	I suppose Echo will be here, too.
Proetus	Yes.
Dorthea	I feel dishonored by my husband.
Proetus	I'm decided you will feel as you must.
Dorthea	Oh, Proetus, your wartime chivalry has wilted on the vine and you with it.
Proetus	We wilt when we can. Will that be all, then?

Dorthea	No. I tell you, I will feel invaded.
Proetus	There is no thought now of bringing her. I go so that we may share our tears and joy at emerging from the den of silence these past forty years.
Dorthea	Best left passed over.
Proetus	I leave at sunrise before the cock crows.
Dorthea	I hear. But the cock will be tardy then.

(Exit Dorthea)

Proetus	(Calling) Echo, Mother!

(Enter Echo from the house)

Must Dorthea have known—

Echo	Of course she knew; I told her.
Proetus	I thank you. What is a mother for? Not perfidy. What is a mother for? Some loyalty. What is a mother who tattles bad news because it excites her to have it aired?
Echo	I have a loyalty to Dorthea also, my dear boy.

Proetus	Well, my dear woman,
	is it blood or sex first, is the issue.
	Sex wins if compulsive revelation
	moves you to reveal my need of Aileen
	to visit. You are on a witch hunt here.

Echo	I don't follow you.

Proetus	True, you don't, Mother.

Echo	Then I am lost.

Proetus	Try following, Echo.
	and avoid your losses. Try thine own son
	as your leader. Address him son, not boy.
	Would our father have looked on this conflict
	as something to savor? I tell you no.
	Would he feature you running to my wife
	with gossip's latest? No again, Mother.
	I urge you to respect him and his son
	before you dabble in cheap rhetoric.

Echo	And now a lecture for your mother.

Proetus	Yes,
	not a talk but lecture. Talks give pleasure;
	lectures, knowledge if the hearer is fit.
	The talk may be informative but fails
	cohesive order that imprints itself
	more lastingly. So you have been lectured,
	not merely talked at.

Echo	I will remember
	your variance and try to learn thereby.

Proetus	Know also that I love you as sons should.

Echo	I stand a bit in awe of that.
Proetus	Mother, I stand in awe of life, its accidents, its expectations, difficulties, ease, the way she wraps her vast arm around us without a warning.
Echo	Oh, Son, you are caught in a labyrinth of old dreams promising new rewards. Beware the Ephetae court; they judge harshly when alerted to sin. Seek out Eos, goddess of our Greek dawn, whose wisdom is bright and great.
Proetus	I will do your counsel if you will keep my station close to you as son who loves you greatly.
Echo	You have the strength of your training in you and the reasoning of Aristotle.
Proetus	Do I have your love?
Echo	Yes, yes, Proetus.

Scene Five. **In the garden plot. Antimodes is seated, waiting. Time: a week later.**

(Enter Tesup)

Tesup

Hey, Antimodes, fancy meeting you
here, but I give up. After a false start
that embarrassed me, I scoured the valleys
for his girlfriend until it dawned on me
that I had looked myself out, moneyless,
and needed returning. How are you here?

Antimodes

Proetus solicited me here, or
I heard a brew had matured, and the mead
was good, Tesup.

Tesup

You have my leg again.

Antimodes

Well, then, you know that retired officers
have some courier service priv'leges,
and he sent me one asking I be here
for whatever reason would escape me
first and, it escaping me, I followed.

Tesup

Either let go my leg or repeat that,
please.

Antimodes

The courier was your friend, Minuss.

Tesup

Well, from Athens and years gone by. Athens.
What was Proetus doing in Athens?

Antimodes

Waiting for a Godot, I think he said.

Tesup

Eh? What's this, this Godot?

Antimodes

You want to know?

Tesup	I quit.
Antimodes	Did you find any candidates?
Tesup	I found a few for me but none, I fear, for Proetus. But I was a good sleuth and enjoyed the work; nothing came of it, is all. I ran into this great beauty in Amphipolis, and mean ran into. I had taken a horse for the trip back, and, turning the mare for the southmost road, ran into this girl so sheltered from sun in a long shawl wound tight around her head that she was blind to the horse. Smack! She fell. Then—
Antimodes	Tesup, rest. I think you must be tired from your efforts. Sit with me.
Tesup	No, not me. I'm not your age, and not expecting soon, either. I can have a woman and walk a mile afterward. Besides, I rested some down yonder.
Antimodes	Rest again then, will you?
Tesup	Antimodes, she was a white beauty, so white from lack of sun that I perspired to think of her. Then when I picked her up, I felt her down and, god, it was all there. Each enjoyed the other in melon beds for an hour. I will sit. Where's Proetus?
Antimodes	He is coming; I was to meet him here.

Tesup	It's a shame we failed him.
Antimodes	Now, as to that—
Tesup	But wasn't that bedrock luck, you old duck? Our southern women would blush to see her, and she was taller than a bald cypress.
Antimodes	Bald cypress! What excellent luck, Tesup.
Tesup	It had nothing to do with simple luck! It had to do with me; a lesser man would have apologized and helped her up without knowing a thing about her and gone his way. No damage for him to lose the prize, but the fool would have deprived her of a noonday clinch, too. Fools will lose it all before a good man can stake his claim. I poked her with my poker when I might, not next week and in my dreams, I tell you.
Antimodes	What if wintertime had frozen the ground and snow began to fall?
Tesup	All the more need for warmth. I would have to dicker with her longer.
Antimodes	But you might need something longer for the haul, no?
Tesup	Who, me?
Antimodes	Yes, you, Tesup.

Tesup	I have a forest down here surrounding one giant spruce bog, man, that elevates at merely thinking girls. Something longer would split my tunic.
Antimodes	I think I'll call you.
Tesup	Meaning what?
Antimodes	Show it, Tesup.
Tesup	I will not.
Antimodes	Show or go home ashamed.
Tesup	What! Ashamed, me?
Antimodes	I believe I discourse with one Tesup.
Tesup	No, sir, I will not show myself to you. You could be a gay fruit sensing a thrill. My god, you could be a number of things. Take the word of an experienced man.
Antimodes	I would, but I will not take yours.
Tesup	So mean that you surprise me. We have been good friends.
Antimodes	That will survive, I promise.
Tesup	But it will be down now.

Antimodes	One of your easier girls, Oenone, says that when it is up it makes no matter, makes no promises, either. What have you for a good woman, Tesup, without garnishing?
Tesup	Between us?
Antimodes	Unconditional surrender.
Tesup	Not much, Antimodes.
Antimodes	This leads to what we call sense in a man's brain, compassion his heart. The item is sensibly over, too; here comes Proetus.
Tesup	Not a word?
Antimodes	Not one.

(Enter Proetus)

Proetus	Oh, Tesup, also. Well, she wasn't yours to find, but all isn't lost, anyway. Antimodes, thank you for meeting me.
Tesup	I looked hard, my friend, but no one had heard of such a woman.
Proetus	But none for yourself?
Tesup	No, my friend.

Proetus	Antimodes, my visit was splendid.
	She was much as I dared think: happy, kind.
	Neither was she lovely as she had been,
	not as full spirited, but time does chew.
	But, by your gods, she was original
	Here are the tetradrachms I promised you;
	late, but why I asked you to oblige me.
Tesup	What?! You found her yourself? How so, old chum?
Proetus	Antimodes: he found her in Athens,
	where all fine Greeks retire to in want of
	finding. Or at least, sir, where he found her.
Antimodes	I tried to tell him, but he unloaded
	his adventures first, and they were lengthy.
	But I think he shares our enthusiasm.
Tesup	Let me be first to say so, both of you.
	It was a great hunt, full of enjoyment.
	I did wear out my face smiling at folks
	I had no reason to smile at, perhaps,
	but I thought a nice smile might get answered
	sooner than a glum puss—and I was right.
	One woman told me she had no notion
	of what I was talking about, but smile
	away, she said, and her house was all mine
	anyway.
Antimodes	But he exited quickly
	that invitation and left for his lunch.
Tesup	I did, my friend.
Proetus	No need to leave eating,
	Tesup. I'll send you thanks for your efforts.

54

Tesup	Well, I thank you, sir. I was ravenous
	while she admired my smile, but I bolted.
	Now I will have to bolt again for home.
	The wife will wait only so long, then feed
	my dinner to the dog. Again, good sir,
	thank you for your kind confidence in me,
	and to you, Anti, I trust you, I hope.

(Exit Tesup)

Proetus	When I knocked on her door, Antimodes,
	I felt a warm flash suffuse my whole face.
	My hand that had knocked began to flutter
	like a giant butterfly, then it stilled.
	I could hardly stand pat, moving around
	like an active child. When I heard her hand
	inside fumbling the latch—it must have slipped—
	a terror seized me. I would have vanished
	had I known how. Your gods know that magic.
	When the door opened, the recognition,
	like knowing enemy, was mutual.
	We embraced before a word was spoken
	and the forty years hiatus dissolved.
	We sputtered loose words at one another,
	each one interfering with excitement
	till calmed. She is a woman I still love
	and will until your gods are all named myths.
	Please forgive me, I can't reduce the child
	in me when thinking of her, I sputter.
	She will be here in some three, four days now.

Antimodes	Your happiness is mine, Proetus. To
	think my work is even a partial cause
	for springing a childhood back into you,
	livening a great maturity, hey,
	I'm Heros, no less, and inclined to brag.

Proetus   Well you may, and for the next lifetime, too.

Antimodes   But—I have no right—

Proetus   You have every right.

Antimodes   Then I have to wonder if Dorthea
                 is at home with all this.

Proetus   No, she is not.
                 It is a damned struggle, I will admit.
                 It is not so difficult for me, though;
                 I simply confess I love two women
                 and blithely whistle off to my schoolyard.

Antimodes   Whistle while you can, Proetus, and luck
                 to you.

Proetus   I will need all you can give me,
                 I know.

Antimodes   To be in love with two women jointly.

Proetus   Not a novelty. Your gods have done it.

Antimodes   Yes, but they have insurance you may lack,
                 sir.

Proetus   Insurance?

Antimodes   Some are returned to life
                 by their relatives or other authors.

Proetus   Then I need to know who is my author.

Antimodes   How would you vote, if on a single night,
                 each little cherub wanted you?

Proetus   No trick.
                    I'm not of an age where I warm the bed,
                    Antimodes.

Antimodes   You warm it if in it,
                    no? Fiery or not, you have blood in you.

Proetus   I do see.

Antimodes   I don't mean to challenge you.

Proetus   Ah, he says, with his longsword at my chest.
                    Then, dear Antimodes, I will follow
                    my dictum of an honest policy,
                    that is, to render truth of the matter
                    to each and lie where matrimony calls.
                    Take down your sword; we have solution here.

Antimodes   Sword stays up till you decide the matter
                    of whose manner most attracts you to bed.

Proetus   The manner if coy or with some warning
                    matters nothing. I will sleep with my wife.

Antimodes   So when you traveled then to your Aileen
                    in Athens—

Proetus   I slept in a public house.

Antimodes   Does Dorthea know this?

Proetus   I believe so.

Antimodes   I would make certain of it, Proetus.

                    **(Enter Dorthea, sitting on the bench which is away
                    from the men)**

Proetus	I will, of course, and thank you profoundly for advice I still find me in need of, Antimodes.
Antimodes	And my full gratitude to you for the excess gift beyond all my expectations, my generous friend.
Proetus	I will keep in touch.

(Exit Antimodes)

(Dorthea is appliquéing, stops and thinks sporadically. Appliqués some more. Finally, desperately, throws the work from her with a small cry of frustration. Several beats. Proetus advances to her.)

Proetus	Dorthea, what is the matter?
Dorthea	Nothing.
Proetus	But why your fine appliqué on the ground?
Dorthea	It must have fallen; it does that when hurt.
Proetus	It feels pain? Well, then, I will pick it up. And you; are you all right with our small world?
Dorthea	Oh, it is small, isn't it? Appliqués are sensitive to it, too, Proetus.
Proetus	I take it, they are.
Dorthea	And balk at some things.

Proetus	Ah, now it comes and we should discuss it, Dorthea. If it continues unsaid, it could cause your weaving another fall.
Dorthea	Let it.
Proetus	Well, poor appliqué, then, my love.
Dorthea	So be it.
Proetus	Poor appliqué, Dorthea.
Dorthea	Oh, that's not it, at all. Not it at all.
Proetus	I know.
Dorthea	How do you? Oh, I know you know. Even Echo knows and the dog will know soon. The slaves remove themselves from the house and play Styx in the courtyard till we end.
Proetus	I would open my whole heart to my wife, if she would have me.
Dorthea	Well, open it then.
Proetus	Dorthea, you have a crucial temper that will uncoil rare and unforeseen times. This woman measures four years of my past in life together, more in influence. I wonder that I let her go, and life went on well for both; but did it, I ask?
Dorthea	But did it?
Proetus	Our times ensure nothing else.

Dorthea   As it does with us?

Proetus   More so; man and wife
               are we by contract.

Dorthea   I wish I could think
               of my need to believe you, but cannot.

Proetus   I am that need! There is no firmer truth!

Dorthea   I have a qualm about this, Proetus.

Proetus   You argue from the pits of behavior
               like lion running from the wildebeest.

Dorthea   What do you mean?

Proetus   I no longer know that.
               But I want you to know that Aileen comes
               in three or four days (her comfort will tell)
               by coach to town and courtesy is pressed
               on you for the stay, brief as it may be.

Dorthea   Ay, that falls like a hammer, Proetus!
               A butterfly would alight more lightly.

Act Two

Scene One.   **In the garden plot. Echo is present, appliquéing.**
Time: three days later.

(Enter Proetus)

Proetus   Mother, where is Dorthea?

Echo   The courtyard.

Proetus   Aileen, if she left as she expected,
           should approach the town shortly.

Echo   And then what?

Proetus   She will rent a good horse from old Biber
           and arrive in an hour. Normally two,
           but, if I know her, she will make it one.
           She is patient but charged with emotion
           and knows I'll be waiting equally charged.
           I know you will relish Aileen as yours
           and help me to negate any unfair
           advantages Dorthea might secure.

Echo   You did repeat your love to Dorthea?

Proetus   I did, and it was like declaring love
           to a willow, all in tears.

Echo	Marvelous.
Proetus	No, nothing to marvel at in this world.
	She would rather defend her poor judgment
	than take twice the time to acknowledge it
	for what it is: hot blood preferred to cold.
	Dorthea's dance has more color enraged
	than if she were to count her every step.
	I have dropped reasoning with her, Mother.
Echo	And I have no more to suggest to you.
Proetus	Maybe luck will find a way with Aileen.
	She has a warmth that victimizes frost,
	which turns to dew, nature's own vapid tear.
	Or so I remember, memory's bank.
	Strange how it resolves at times and then not.
Echo	Strange, too, how our eye resolves and then not.
	Someone astride a horse, I would venture,
	has just entered the valley's farthest side,
	though it's too soon to know on horse or ass.
Proetus	It could be Aileen but, right, it's too soon.
	My two-decade-younger eye fails that test
	also, but our Aegean sun splatters
	the image.
Echo	How has our good neighbor, Rome,
	Worked out the coming of her nemesis,
	Hannibal?
Proetus	The Carthage general, known
	for his field skills, not love of elephants,
	lost all but one animal, winning big
	against Rome's legions but not Rome herself.

Meantime, the Carthaginian floundered
and, back in Gaul, has been sent to protect
his capital. A hard war is his now.

Echo   The dear boy is too young for his army.

Proetus   His army hardly thinks so.

Echo   His army,
Pah! Pah!

Proetus   Well trained and armed, those Carthage boys.

Echo   They are still boys.

Proetus   Old men don't do so well
in the field anymore. Fancy me gone
to war again. One must drive chariots
with speed, resolve, minding your shield, your sword.
Your boys will whip your old man every time.
I still can't see for seeing that distance.
Another reduction of means: eyesight.

Echo   You will still do, in a pinch, I wager.

Proetus   Then send me off to a pinch, no more war.

Echo   I'll send you off nowhere.

Proetus   (Looking to the valley)
                             The sun, my foe.
But look, Mother, does that orb circle us,
or do we encircle it? Which one, now,
is stable? Or is neither body that?
Do they revolve or stay stationary
in their orbit; do we stay or revolve?
I tell you, we have much yet to digest;

63

when we do, however, let the world watch.
Athens will rule it. If not her nation,
her spirit will, her knowledge and her arts,
her record of democracy, Mother.
We are greatness!

Echo   Oh, hide your head in shame.

Proctus   No, there is no shame in Athens' greatness.
               And I see our animal is a horse,
               our rider an Athenian woman
               of considered riding skill who saddles
               to the side and, I think, should be Aileen.
               We are in fact all greatness, dear Mother,
               in this moment and all ensuing ones.

Echo   Where will she leave her tired horse, Proetus?

Proetus   In our barn to be limed by the swallows.
               She is almost there now and will be here
               shortly. I hope the two of you agree
               to like one another or, battle lost,
               you will occupy the farthest chamber.

Echo   Oh, well, Son, she can't be that difficult
               to be fond of. She pleased you, after all.
               I'm beginning to feel somewhat calmer
               now that she's here.

Proetus   Things will get smoother still.

Echo   But you would, would you, move your own mother
               so that your lady might find more comfort
               in her surroundings?

Proetus   I would move heaven
               and earth for her.

64

Echo	Those, too?
Proetus	Those, too, Mother.
Echo	Oh, dear, when a man is smitten, he's cooked to the way you would want him, I suppose.
Proetus	She's in the barn. There is a fresh stall there with hay and water for the animal.
Echo	And for her?
Proetus	Water, mirror and a brush.
Echo	Well thought out, my boy.
Proetus	Women's provisions. She's here.

(Enter Aileen)

Proetus	Aileen, my mother, Echo. Do sit down.
Aileen	I would like to stand a moment.
Proetus	Of course,
Echo	I am most pleased to welcome you, Aileen.
Aileen	Much has been recounted about Echo, the well loved member of her family.
Echo	(Flustered) Oh, tut.

Proetus   (To Echo)
                          It's a platform you must stand on.
                 Aileen has heard of nearly everyone.
                 We are momentous without heavy weight.

Echo   His tank is very full of you, madam.
                 He says he loves you and we know he does.
                 He also loves his wife; we know he does,
                 too. He would love a Persian, I believe,
                 if the thing stood over him with knife drawn.

Aileen   I know of this and would desire to woo
                 anyone to us who could not grasp us.
                 We don't supplant a soul or good system
                 long in place. Neither one is young enough
                 to strike fear at any institution.
                 That in itself does guarantee safety
                 to us. And remaining love for his wife
                 is further safety. Why, the guarantees
                 are so numerous you can't fault them all.
                 No horse is guaranteed not to stumble
                 or throw his rider, yet we still ride them.

Echo   I like this woman, Proetus, she speaks
                 to the point!

Proetus   I said she would; remember?

Echo   No such thing. I arrived at liking her
                 myself.

Proetus   Quite right; you are always quite right.

Echo   No such thing there, either. I'm not quite right
                 always. Rarely am I, if truth be known.

Proetus	But I think we are respectful of that and should join Dorthea where we find her.
Echo	One moment more, my boy, a quick moment that will set my heart at ease.
Proetus	Well, one, then.
Echo	My son is married. That you know, respect and have set aside for good observance. I have not heard you say in plain language that you don't covet him for yours.
Proetus	Mother—
Aileen	That's a fair request, Proetus, most fair. We seem to avoid the simplest wordings for the intents we harbor to ourselves and leave some doors open that your mother wants closed. I want them closed also.
Echo	Firmly.
Aileen	Yes, firmly. And I say to you, Echo, that I loved your son, Proetus, firmly once and do again but differently. We cannot enjoy the physic of love as once we did for two topside reasons: his marriage does prohibit it, and I, as I did with my own, honor that pact.
Echo	(To Proetus) Well, she is right to the point, Proetus. I love her as I do our Dorthea.
Aileen	Then like your son, you must love two women jointly.

Echo   And you say that my son could, too.

Aileen   Yes, Echo; I am not a hypocrite.

Proetus   We must go inside and introduce you
to Dorthea. She will be in the yard
expecting us. Are we ready, Mother?

Echo   You know I am.

| Scene Two. | **In the living room. Present are Proetus and Aileen.** |
| | **Time: a few minutes later.** |

Aileen   Proetus, I begin to feel angry
with myself for coming into your home.
It was unwise to impose my person
on a wife who we know to be jealous.
She is within the rights of her marriage
to object to me.

Proetus   Within her rights, too,
to accept you, to know and to love you.

Aileen   Then why do I feel this uneasiness?

Proetus   For a one day stay, I can't imagine. It may all wash
away when Echo comes
back from the courtyard towing Dorthea.
As the sun warms a battlefield before
it runs red and fleshed, Echo seeks comfort
in Dorthea so that anger is lost
and reason at least flirted with. Flirted,
mind you.

Aileen   You told me in Athens of none
of this. You told me she would take her time
but, given that, there would be amnesty.

Proetus   Precisely; she is now taking her time.

Aileen   Oh, my goodness.

Proetus   I did exaggerate
the ease with her, but I was and am sure
that I know a wife of twenty-some years.

Aileen   Well, we shall see.

Proetus	Trust, my love.

Aileen	Proetus,
	trust and honor are my good bed-fellows;
	I must not you and so I sleep with them.
	And you, sir, must watch your close endearments;
	love is what we all must have for us all.

Proetus	They're coming. And what time will she take now?

(Enter Echo and Dorthea)

Echo	The tulips are thriving in the garden.
	Dorthea, I want you to meet Aileen.
	Aileen, Dorthea.

Dorthea	Pleased, I assure you.

Aileen	And no more can I do to assure you
	than to press your hand with my heavy heart;
	it will be unburdened when friendship blooms.

Echo	That's a good thing said to you, Dorthea.

Dorthea	Yes, it is.

Echo	Well, we must be comforted
	by seating.
	(They sit)

Proetus	Here, Dorthea, your fav'rite
	chair. Yours, Echo.

Echo	Yes, thank you.

Proetus	And Aileen.

Aileen	Thank you.
Proetus	(A chair for himself) The chairs are heavy but well made; All done some time ago by my father.
Echo	I helped, I remember.
Proetus	Yes.
Echo	A little.
Proetus	Well, you made the hefty cushions, Mother.
Echo	I did, with our Dorthea's help.
Proetus	Yes, yes.
Aileen	Lovely cushions, too.
Echo	Appliquéd, also.
Aileen	Yes.
Proetus	So much for the chairs, then (beat). And the cushions (beat). And the appliqué.
Echo	Yes, the appliqué was a difficult design, leaves and stems.
Proetus	I have always sat with anxiety believe me, in so much rough shrubbery.
Aileen	Perhaps it would be best if I begin: I had always admired this Proetus but feared losing him to his profession

so that, when I left, I felt some relief
to be serving a good peaceful bus'ness
with proven duration. Life is shortened
in wartime, and I could not have carried
his omission in me. Best not to know
his death in battle if it should occur.
Then, too, I met a man who courted me,
and I was pleased to marry him. Oh, yes,
he was thoughtful, generous as a man
could be, and we lived well for forty years.
When he died, I was left with relatives
who filled the hours, but time became heavy
with his absence until a messenger
from Proetus came lifting boredom's veil.
Forty years had passed and now new meaning
struck a cymbal and trumpeted its way
into an old life, well enough and fit
to receive it. Should I have declined him?
To what purpose turn away a value?
A sot in his liquors will ignore it.
A strumpet too concerned with herself will.
I did not and will not turn this meaning
from my door, this kind, final adventure.
Who has, in a lifetime, found incident
like it? I wish it were everyone's own.

Echo   Well said, Dorthea. Or what do you think?

Dorthea   She speaks well.

Echo   I thought so, too, from Athens.

Proetus   Oh, well, that Athens has its voices there.
                That fellow, Plato, wields a stirring tongue
                affixed, I think, to a sometime geniused
                pair of lips collecting new disciples
                daily. He is the hit among sophists
                everywhere.

Echo	Yes, he writes volumes, he does, on everything from numbers, politics and thinking to poetics. He speaks well, they say. There are quite a few nameless ones I can't remember.
Dorthea	I should have more time—
Proetus	We all should, Dorthea. I do agree.
Aileen	Time is no shipload but a whole navy to us women.
Dorthea	Oh, I could second that!
Proetus	But you still manage a well ordered home, Dorthea.
Dorthea	I try.
Echo	And success is yours, ducky.
Proetus	Yet, lest our horse gets lost again, we should rein him in and onto his track. Aileen has with honesty and courage delivered you to her encounter's pain and joy, no easy task to her nature. Nor has it been easy for Dorthea to hear and formulate some good answer to a situation strange and hostile to her, one that challenges her fiber.
Echo	Yes, let's get onto it with dignity and purpose and, as said, with some reining and purpose, then some sense of direction.

Aileen	If it suits one, I would answer a point.
Dorthea	I would ask one then: Do you love this man?
Proetus	Dorthea, that is not—

Aileen

                             Yes, Proetus
it is a fair point and will get answered.
When you question depth in my emotion
I must confess I neither know nor see
it matters, since I do respond to him.
He sent a messenger I hardly thought
could tell truth from fiction, but who so urged
my belief in him that whole acceptance
of his mission ensued. Then the visit
by Proetus followed. Who could deny
that tandem? When recognition followed,
so did remembrances sprout and blossom
like azalea. A forest of that flow'r
surrounded us till he left and Eros
designed to stay. Submit yourself to that
two visits and ask, are you stunned, in love
or disgusted with the air you breathe?
I have given more than a fair answer;
it was a description of my passion.
Call it love or another affliction.

Dorthea

Oh, I must confess to great confusion.
Your answers are adroit, making questions
often seem foolish, and I do not mean
them to be. I am at sea in all this.

Echo

You are at home and comfortable, daughter.

Proetus

I love you, Dorthea, and will always.

Dorthea	Yes, but why must you and Echo sound me so often with your love and affection? Do I look weak or in need of support? I am in my home as you, Echo, note and am comfortable in my common way; why do you patronize me, dear Mother?
Proetus	Oh, she is no patron to you, my love.
Dorthea	And you, too, patronize me, Proetus.
Proetus	Do I?
Dorthea	I think you do.
Proetus	Then I will quit, because it's not my object to rile you. My only object is to let you know I love my wife and the role is well filled.
Echo	And I may be patronizing, dear girl, but will erase the slate and use caution in future. Count on it, my dear angel.
Dorthea	There! You angeled me.
Echo	I'll devil you next and confusion will reign on Olympus, I tell you.
Proetus	More questions from my wife now.
Dorthea	(To Aileen) When you stay here or anywhere, you sleep alone, I take it.
Aileen	Alone is seemly.

Dorthea   Then this question is to you, Proetus.
               Will you love this woman as you do me?

Proetus   No. No two love-nests are identical,
               Dorthea. What one woman holds most dear,
               another may abhor. If their perfumes
               are similar, then chance visited them.
               I can only love you as you quicken
               my life, as you love me for like assigns.
               I have eaten at both your fine tables
               and will not compare them; they are diff'rent
               as two elegiacs, two quadrupeds
               or, if you will allow me, two women,
               two men or two asses. Now we are down
               to it, incomparable, do you see?

Dorthea   If it fell to you to have to make choice
               an evening, to sleep in her bed or mine—
               how would you choose, Husband?

Proetus   Sleep on the floor
               is evasive answering, I know, Wife,
               but discretionary, too.

Dorthea   Ay, you rat!
               You are strong enough to do it, I think!

Proetus   Bet on it; I am not walking in muck
               the rest of my life!

Dorthea   Well, the question was
               unfair, I suppose.

Proetus   So was the answer.

76

Dorthea	But I cannot help being suspicious of a husband with such long memory. Why would he cherish such a reflection for so long, eh, and seek her out, at that? Why her and not another? Answer that. Do I hear a long answer, Proetus?
Proetus	Neither long nor a short one, Dorthea.
Dorthea	Yes, neither long nor short of it, Husband. Why this one among many, and I'm sure a fine captain would have his pick often of the fair and the unfair, his choices. Why this one, this Aileen, of forty years? Did she make his bed a revelation?
Proetus	That is unfair and not in too good taste.
Dorthea	But is this whole affair in the best taste, Husband?
Proetus	Does this occur so often, Wife, that taste exists for it in our morals? If so, tell me the tale of one other known to you and we will give it its taste. My thought is they will both deny bad taste.
Dorthea	I may have picked the wrong word, Proetus.
Proetus	Picking the right one is often a task, I know, but shorter time is given rein. Brevity is king; the wrong word, joker, but we all murder kings and joke our lives away now or some later, do we not? I don't know what the right word is, my love, but must deny a value to your taste. Let us move on, then.

Dorthea	Move on to what, please?
Proetus	Oh, well, to the next road we intersect.
Echo	Proetus, you engage in ridicule. That is not the purpose of this meeting.
Proetus	I meant we move to whatever conjoins. But, Dorthea, I think it wise to strike suggestions as to what conduct we think may have happened some forty years ago. Who knows what did happen; no one will know.
Dorthea	Her quick visit is for one day only. I am fixed. Why her and not another?
Proetus	None other came upon me with such force. She told me how to live with a bad wound without traces and gave me vast insight into a problem dominating me at that time.
Dorthea	What problem?
Proetus	Can't remember. Or, if you permit my telling these folks your terrible quandary of ten, twelve years gone, I might remember to your pleasure.
Dorthea	Ay! I see you mean to hide it from me! Keep it, then.
Proetus	Fair enough, I will keep it.
Aileen	Dorthea, are you done with me for now?

Dorthea   No, no, madam, with you I am not done.
Though I do appreciate your candor
and the depths of your discussion, I won't
say that I am finished with you quite yet.
It is a marvelous journey you take
to come here, and I'll see you given care
and the courtesy you deserve, madam.
If I fail, I'm sure Proetus will not.
And, Husband, we will talk more of this soon.

Echo   Well, I smell our dinner from the courtyard.

Dorthea   Tomorrow I will go to the market
and if you wish, Echo, you may go, too.
Yes, we will have a new chick in the nest
and must take care for her timely fledging.

Echo   I'll be pleased to go with you, Dorthea,
but now let's eat.

Scene Three.   **In a nearby wooded area. Present are Proetus and Aileen. Time: the following day.**

Proetus: This is the place I mentioned in Athens.
It was cut and cleared by my dear father
as a refuge from the cares of the world.
He would come and look for animal scat
and retire to the bench, listening
to birdsong. Often he came before light
even to hear what one calls dawn chorus
son. "The awakening of the planet,"
he called it. It was his private temple.
Proetus has been its only tenant
since. There, the foliated set is gone;
sit, Aileen. It was his own Parthenon,
designed for feeling and contemplation.
He said it restored his faith in himself,
and he taught me be fearless of the gods.

Aileen   I am honored, but I will fear my gods
so when Zeus hears of it he will be pleased.

Proetus   If I were Zeus, I would be pleased with you
whatever your conviction.

Aileen   Proetus,
let's dwell on us. We are alone now, love.

Proetus   Yes, after forty years.

Aileen   A miracle
and two months, I figure.

Proetus   Really, two months?

Aileen	An eternity with an intention,
	it seems, as though happy life with one man
	could afford me the one and one more still.
	It is the most romantic thought of all
	that afterlife may yet be spent alive
	and in Greece where life is so familiar,
	where there are trees, large bodies of water,
	columned buildings with floored or walled motifs
	of Tritons and Nereids figured.
	Oh, of all my gods, Proetus exceeds
	the lot in that he's the most flattering:
	he comes in chariot, then so in flesh
	that no woman can look the other way.
Proetus	I am near pushing seventy, Aileen,
	and closer yet to meek embarrassment.
Aileen	I call it as I see it, my good sir.
	The list continues: he is too civil
	for some courts and so languid in his speech
	that dolphins listen enraptured to him.
Proetus	Oh, I beg for time out to object, please.
Aileen	Why, do you object to the grateful state
	you find me in? I could go on, you know,
	since endings seem so out of fashion here.
	I am a widow, you know, a few years
	from remorse and capable, you will find,
	of a woman's eye for continued life.
	You propose it and I do accept, sir.
Proetus	It is all too sweet for my diet, love.

Aileen	It is not too sweet for my lover, though. He is all that my imagination can embrace: the too ripe, the scurrilous, all fit because he is the everyman of life without ending. That is your crown. Wear it.
Proetus	I will, whether it fits or not.
Aileen	Oh, put it on at some dapper angle and it will fit your other countenance.
Proetus	I'm dapper now? You should tell my mother.
Aileen	That is not something one tells one's mother.
Proetus	You are more joy than a monkey barrel.
Aileen	I am very glad you find me joyful.
Proetus	I know whom I hunted when I hunted. And already I resent my using so much of active life that I crumble beside you. I am not the man you knew.
Aileen	You have made war and lived to pursue me. Would you humble yourself before me, too?
Proetus	Any time before you, my precious thing. Listen. That's a song you should memorize, the warble of the chaffinch, ten notes long. There, again, by him or by another.
Aileen	Well, I have it.
Proetus	Then sing it back to him.

Aileen   (Attempts to duplicate the song)

Proetus   Not bad.

Aileen   It was terrible!

Proetus   Terrible,
                then, but it will shore up your memory
                of it. You are ringed in pristine timbre;
                all manner of birds put up their nests here.
                The finch you heard is almost regular.
                Ah, and there! You hear a warbler singing.

Aileen   What? That chiff-chaff noise?

Proetus   Precisely, chiff-chaff.

Aileen   Is that all he does, and you say warble?

Proetus   I think that's all.

Aileen   That is not a warble.
                The other bird, the chaffinch, did warble.
                Your warbler is a fraud, should be renamed.

Proetus   I will take it up—

Aileen   Take it up with whom?

Proetus   Search me. Flip a drachm, but if the owl
                appears, he will eat both birds anyway,
                and problem will be solved. By a small owl,
                no less.

Aileen   Owls eat songbirds.

Proetus   Ones they can catch.

Aileen	Well, you have caught me. Are you an owl?
Proetus	Who.

Who. I'm a little owl come to catch you.
I'll pellet and disgorge you at the foot
of my imaginings, yes, at the foot
of my ardor and my love. No escape
for you whatever, my tasty morsel.

Aileen	No thought of escape here, indiscreet owl.
Proetus	Why indiscreet?

Aileen
                                  Because your hunger is.
For one thoughtless feed you will sacrifice
dining again here.

Proetus
                         True, I must figure
somehow to reincarnate your first form,
your loveliest semblance, a well-shaped mien
to something other than a wee warbler.
I ponder.

Aileen	You must think hard, little owl.
Proetus	I shall.

Aileen
                  It is a fun game you enter
me into.

Proetus
                  That's it! I may only come
to enter into you as a wee owl
like myself. Therefore, birds of a feather
have more fun together. Did I do that
with some tact, d'you think?

Aileen   Some, but not enough.

Proetus   Oh, why, love?

Aileen   We are committed by age
               and contract to celibacy.

Proetus   Well, yes,
               but there's no more than pure love which we own.

Aileen   The eight years spent between my husband's death
               and your discovering me were white years
               blanked between a colorful and full time,
               lavender and purple, given to work
               and play, and your Athenian finding
               of a forty-year-old, worn and tattered
               adoration soon colored purest gold.
               This is the quintessence, sir, of romance.

Proetus   You are just a few years older than I,
               far from worn and just a little tattered,
               by my eye. My mountain of memory
               places you in youth yet. There you remain.

Aileen   But, my dear man, do you know how you must
               fill a woman's life?

Proetus   How you top off mine,
               I would think. If climax has one more drift,
               my dear, I think you'd find their meanings close.

Aileen   I do, I do, Proetus. They are close.
               Words, while they mount such impressive soundings
               of our feelings, do record them for us.

Proetus   What for meaning is involved in that speech,
               golden one?

Aileen	I'm unsure, but make a claim for some originality in it.
Proetus	Now deep, the bow plunges into the trough.
Aileen	Can you navigate such waters, my love?
Proetus	Merely try. My life was military.
Aileen	Well, send a scout.
Proetus	Lady, I know nothing of our direction, and the wind is up.
Aileen	Oh, never ask the militant to sail in a weather threatening to confuse. Ask someone else, any passing body— A tall man of good countenance and lean—
Proetus	Put a stop to that I will, and quickly.
Aileen	So, stopped then; where to next, languid lover? Do you remember our oldest pleasure when I returned from walking with sore feet? It was a joy to us both, I recall.
Proetus	I don't remember that one.
Aileen	Do you not?
Proetus	I will try it again in my good time.
Aileen	Now is a good time. When I came indoors and began massaging my tired feet you would suggest I sit, and from a stool anointed one and then the other foot. It was a most refreshing thing you did.

Proetus	It was?
Aileen	Yes, it made my whole leg feel new.
Proetus	Oh, now I think I have it: the foot rub!
Aileen	Yes.
Proetus	I loved to do it! I was thrilled by it.
	Somehow I was moved by it and by you,
	challenged then in a way I can't summon.
	There, we will have a foot massage. Sit back.
	I'll take your sandals, and you relax now.
	How could I ever forget a pleasure?

(He begins to massage her feet, one foot first)

Aileen	I think the four years we lived together
	you performed this no less than thirty times,
	and each time was better than the other.
	It is why the musician practices,
	I guess. I'm surprised you failed to call up
	that one, you were so fond of doing it.
	Or so you said.
Proetus	I do recollect now.
	In a time of afternoon or evening,
	I would think of it even before you.
Aileen	Yes.
Proetus	You were the only woman in the world
	who could make this substantial warrior
	servile. My commander had no more sway.
	What you provided: warmth, intelligence,
	uncommon industry made a man feel
	greatly composed and strikingly serene.
	Why would that man not bend his knee to you?

Aileen	You are very kind.
Proetus	And you, my love, blessed and Elysian.
Aileen	For a man without gods you say, blessed?
Proetus	I say anything I please to confirm a value, get above truth, with truth in the mix.
Aileen	Always the deep one, you needed a sword's thrust into language in order to bleed forth an absolute. I see no change in the fine man I've loved.
Proetus	Very little but age.
Aileen	Were you sorry when I had to leave?
Proetus	Not sorry; vacant. The sorrow was spent in new tasks, busy and sometimes hollow business, fresh tunics and the like. I tried to replace you; failed. I forgot you and then I remembered. Forgot again and tried to replace you. Failed. The circle was dizzying and dense. Still I tried. And then I would remember. I met vital women needing husbands. Failed them all. I was a poor citizen and was not near the man I was with you. The bold tidal waters were at my feet, lapping, withdrawing, teasing, calling me to beware the breaker, one that would sting

and crack all consciousness with my living.
Death was close to me for all one's reckless,
wayward adventuring down darkened shores.
I lost a good conflict, then another
and so lost all hope of winning my way.
I, knowing you had married, knew also
that I must win my next conflict in life,
which I did to my amusement and pain.
Pain and amusement, then, became my life,
and I wallowed in it like the breakers.

Aileen   You had a difficult time, Proetus,
                while I found comfort and satisfaction
                in a good man's arms.

Proetus   As I always felt
                you must have, and I gave myself credit
                in both columns for my success in that.
                It was a joke on me that I carried,
                no real consciousness of the droll humor.
                I felt like a wealthy philanthropist
                who had given a great woman value
                in the land's coin to equal her greatness.

Aileen   You overestimate me, Proetus.

Proetus   I have never and do not do that now.

Aileen   Oh, how I have missed your great honesty.

Proetus   Oh, I suppose, and how I have missed you.
                Nothing must separate us, not again.

Aileen   Nothing but the grave will, my loving word.

Proetus	For now, I'm too content to advantage I do have over madam's lovely feet. On this toe you have a little bunion, though.
Aileen	Nothing less than that toe's love for you.
Proetus	I see no ingrown nails; here a blister that has expressed and gone its merry way.
Aileen	Your hands feel very good, Captain.
Proetus	Stop that. We're lovers of equally good fortune. Having done our stints in life, we reason this to be another one free of names, titles, and endowments, full of pleasure, thought and the manifold acts we dream of in that first life unkindly not left us.
Aileen	My love, you are some above the ankle.
Proetus	Well, yes.
Aileen	I just wanted you to know that.
Proetus	I go up from the foot and then back down. Surely that was the way I did before. Doesn't it feel good?
Aileen	It feels very good.
Proetus	When you want me to stop, oh, just tell me.
Aileen	Yes, I will, I will.
Proctus	I do enjoy it.

Aileen   I am that happy benefactor, too.

Proetus   I could go to your knee, if you want me.

Aileen   Well, our ages dictate—

Proetus   We'll do that then.
                (He does)

Aileen   Oh.

Proetus   The feeling is good for me, if for you.
                You are surprisingly firm for your age.

Aileen   Oh, I know, I know.

Proetus   Are you still all right?

Aileen   I am all right. Are you sure you did this
                before?

Proetus   Positive. I remember now
                the whole bit. How did I lose thought of it?

Aileen   Ah.
                (She is affected)

Proetus   I went to the thigh then.
                (But he does not)

Aileen   Proetus!

Proetus   How I love you and will venerate you
                and reroute your whole future into me,
                mine into you. It is a life dessert
                not common to the species, dear Aileen.
                (He is aroused also)

Aileen	My dear!
Proetus	In my hand, the oyster enshelled!
Aileen	Stop, love, stop! (It is too late)
Proetus	Ah, ah! (They complete together and rest)
Aileen	You're surprising, love. (Time, beats)
Proetus	We are restive record makers, my dear. (Time, beats) Do you know that forty-some years ago, we did the same thing but more completely? It was our very first time together.
Aileen	I do remember.
Proetus	We watched the sunrise.
Aileen	It was a golden time, those early years. Everything was easier: an arm moved without worry, our weight was set upon a leg with trust, all our toes were supple, and the body worked to quick perfection. How does your fine corpus relate to you?
Proetus	Not often enough but still serves me well. I think of the body as more baggage, best used for the expression of our love and making war but, when I refigure, I find that eating an apple or date becomes an imposing problem.

Aileen	At least.

Proetus

Then when I began to think well of me,
I lost some hair, sprained an ankle or hand,
got the gout or fought wrinkles in my hands.
It all came to something else, and daily.
The able flesh attacked and left one crouched,
leg flesh fell, so softened, slowed my quick walk.
It is a miracle that none of this
happens to our gods. They go on useful
for centuries, no disability,
no pain. I've always wanted to be one.

Aileen

You have already done that lofty thing.

Proetus

Yes, in pursuit of you, I am lofty.

Aileen

But what if failure had been the result?

Proetus

I would have lived out my life in a bowl
of ordinary failures, successes
and memories. Nothing to strut about.
Well, my love, shall we move to return now?

Aileen

Well, yes, we should, of course, though circumspect,
halted, thinking forces me to conclude
on this: despite a stable and valued marriage
of length, you have kept in your mind's closet
a notion of me. This confirmation
is of some int'rest. It describes either
a man worn by marriage seeking other
freshening probes or him whose whole visage
is love's turnstile from which, it may be said,
there is no exit. You, that latter man,
bore my image through life's frenzied tumult
without doubt or loss or rancor, anger,

grief or gesture of despair. Is that so?
Because just one of those would erase me.
Whatever you are not, you are my man,
Proetus, of the most consummate love
a woman could aspire to. Shall we now?

Scene Four.   **In the garden plot. Present are Proetus, Aileen and Dorthea. Time: next morning.**

Dorthea   Lesia was not enough for the trip,
              so I brought in Kio to give a hand.
              Two slaves, I thought, would give us sufficient
              portage for what I needed on the trip,
              and in the market I saw that Kio
              was gone, our wonderful and kind Kio.
              Well, you know our police are also slaves,
              and the one I asked to find him declined—
              saying Kio would be found. He knew him!

Proetus   If Kio slipped, he will pay with his life,
              so there'll be no recurrence of the act.
              I'm glad you could find a cart to load up
              and got things home. I will miss brave Kio
              if desertion was his object. Confound,
              he was a strong field hand.

Dorthea   And courteous.
              But did you spend your time well with Aileen?

Proetus   You might ask her that.

Dorthea   I thought I asked you.

Proetus   I thought it well spent. We spoke and listened,
              each exhausting the other with stories,
              anecdotes, trivia, rank foolishness.
              It was a time of little discov'ries,
              not histories or lengthy platitudes.
              Her husband was a thoughtful man, I learned.

Aileen   I threw the discus a decameter,
              I told him, but that was some years ago.

Dorthea   You did that? I never heard of woman
             doing that long distance with the discus.

Aileen   I quit responsibly thereafter, so
             to end the game on a strong note, not one
             of weakness. I turned to something other
             like appliqué, if I can remember.

Dorthea   From the discus to needles, imagine!
             I know you are older than Proetus.

Aileen   Yes, by some twelve years.

Dorthea   Ah, not by twelve years!
             I heard by three or four; that I believe!

Proetus   Aileen, you've said twelve years separate us;
             why such a gross and fictional number?

Aileen   I said twelve?

Proetus   You did.

Dorthea   You said twelve, all right.

Aileen   Well, I beg your pardon. I have errors
             built into age, I fear. Never condoned,
             I still must understand their good purpose
             if they have one, and that grasp eludes me.
             I hope you forgive.

Proetus   Nothing to forgive,
             Aileen. We all have little oddities
             imposed on us by age, but never twelve
             years of them when a three or four will do.

Dorthea	I am nine years younger than Proetus, and if you were twelve older, I would be your junior by twenty-one years, lady. Haw, but your four years will give us only thirteen, and the leg-up will still be mine. You do know how I refer to leg-up, my dear?
Aileen	The clear opposite of hands down, I take it, or, if not, some better thing laid out on silk sheets for some stout fellow.
Dorthea	Oh, yes, that would top the leg-up picture. Tell me more about your fair yesterday: did you say nice things to one another, recite Pindar or Aristophanes?
Proetus	It was poetic but with no Pindar, Dorthea.
Dorthea	You say. How says the lady?
Aileen	No Pindar.
Dorthea	And no Aristophanes?
Aileen	Oh, I believe you mean to rattle me.
Dorthea	Yes, yes, I would rattle you if I could.
Aileen	But you cannot.
Dorthea	Well, I believe I can. Proetus has scrolls of both those poets, but he knows much by heart of both of them. It reasons that he would have quoted one or the other to you in the day's time.

Proetus	Those poets I quoted you, Dorthea.
	They are not used for conquering the world.
Dorthea	Who asked you? I addressed the lady here.
Aileen	No poetry.
Proetus	No more inquisition,
	either, Dorthea. You lack the license
	and the good manners both, and I ask you
	do put down such churlish hostility
	more appropriate for an enemy
	than friend. I'll have no more of it, you hear?
Dorthea	I make no enemy of the lady,
	insofar as I can tell it, Husband.
	She has not cried help or asked assistance
	from you. Why would you offer it, I ask?
	She's my friend as well as our honored guest.
Proetus	That gives a better sound to everything.
Dorthea	Then I would ask the lady another
	question, one out of simple ignorance,
	since it hasn't happened to me for years:
	had you the good fortune to hold his hand?
Proetus	A quick, uncivil question, Dorthea.
	You are making it difficult for me
	to maintain the role I must: constable
	of fairness between two women I love.
	Help me, please, to be successful at it.
Dorthea	To the best of my ability, then.

Aileen	I never once gave thought to hold his hand but, had I, the thing would have been performed without a witness, if that's your concern.
Dorthea	Ay! Where were you that you lacked witnesses?
Proetus	Where we wished to be, and not your concern!
Dorthea	You were certainly seated, not upright for all that time together, were you not?
Proetus	Yes, of course.
Dorthea	Well, then, either in the house or here, which?
Proetus	The bench was chosen, hands down.
Dorthea	Yet this bench is public to our Echo and to passing slaves. Would you hold hands here? I think no. There are only two more seats: one in the valley which is not private and the one in Father's woods! Whoa, my gods! You could do anything there, my sweethearts!
Proetus	But we did not do what you fantasize. We discussed the many years, her marriage and mine. We spent a while on songbirds, too. They sang for us, and she denied their names were chosen well or something about them that wasn't right and—I don't remember.
Dorthea	However, you were there!

Proetus	My father's bench!
	What is the matter with you, woman? I
	am full to here with your petty nonsense
	and interrogations meaning nothing
	but a suspect wife with no credentials.
	Take a hike down the path to the valley
	and note the hollyhocks, the sunflowers,
	that turn their faces to the sun; do it
	and regulate your anger according
	to the new warmth within you. Do it now!
Dorthea	As you are my master, I must obey.
	But I do, like all Greek women, deplore
	the sun's effects and seek your permission
	to go to the house instead.
Proetus	To the house,
	then, but no wine and no mead for the day.
Aileen	Dorthea, wait. No reason emerges
	in my mind for your going. Proetus
	and I have not done what you fear we do,
	and will not in the future. Shall I fear
	the two of you performing likewise? No.
	It is your god given and legal right.
	My int'rest in this man was primary
	to yours. It was his need to let me go
	when time afforded him no keeping way.
	He would return to war. Now forty years
	into time, I have the chance to see him
	again as mine, if not all but somewhat.
	Should I shun him? Would you? I believe not.
	Thus, I have his friendship and gifted love.
	An extra grain of luck, I might have yours.
Dorthea	You wish to have me compromised, my dear.

Aileen	No, but I like "dear" better than "lady."
Dorthea	You are such a strange idea to me, though. You are the opposite of my safety in this marriage.
Aileen	But how so?
Dorthea	You exist! You have been in love with my Proetus, and real love does not extinguish, I think.
Aileen	I agree with you, and now we must know it is the same for lucky Proetus.
Dorthea	No! I hesitate there. If he loves me, he cannot love another. That is firm thought in my book.
Aileen	But what limits his love?
Dorthea	Ha! I do!
Aileen	Then one's love is limited by one who receives it. There is no more. The well is dry and cannot be re-used, is that so?
Dorthea	That's the way I reckon it.
Aileen	Had you no sweet children in your marriage who would receive your love and affection?
Dorthea	We were too old then.
Aileen	Ah, it's a pity.

Dorthea	Say, what's a pity?
Aileen	They could have loved you. But then, the well being dry, they would lose their loves for later loves and marriages. So in your book, our man, first loving me, he cannot have loved you for twenty years. His well is dry.
Dorthea	I knew there would be grief here should you come. So I'll consult my gods and make their answer to you also mine.
Aileen	They may answer only what you wish heard.
Dorthea	But I will know them; I do not know you.
Preotus	Please, Dorthea, they are not good guidons.
Dorthea	And sometimes I think I do not know you.

(Exit Dorthea into the house)

Proetus	When she's angry, she has left her softness and her mind to the Furies. When she leaves her company, she finds it too much pain to bear and retreats to safer quarters. She is a good woman, Aileen, immersed in a strange world of haughty argument, ineducable and intransigent as Gibraltar; still, in her way, goodness.
Aileen	I know her for a good woman and wife. I'll go have another word with her now.
Proetus	No, let it rest. Dorthea will smolder a while and return as though no debate occurred.

Aileen	But she is a wounded sparrow needing comfort. Let me attend to her, and I will bring her back hale and cordial.
Proetus	She will bring those qualities unaided within minutes.
Aileen	Then I'll practice restraint.
Proetus	I love that woman; it's well you know that since it reinforces our own union, bringing truth to the fore in all of us. Dorthea's anger was discomforting to both, but it will have had catharsis in it for all, I promise it, Aileen.
Aileen	You know her best.
Proetus	Often I think that's so, but when the light of new day dawns, I doubt the whole fortress of my thinking on it. I see my whimsy against a black cloud and beg the day to enter night again. Oh, that same night that closed on Hannibal at Carthage and slew both that great city and its youthful leader. Rome took it all, I hear. Will I take a small advantage?
Aileen	You are the only man to entertain Dorthea for the time of twenty years. That time is yours, and the knowledge thereby is yours, and no man knows her better, sir.
Proetus	You may not always be right, but gods' wrath, you may be always a cozy comfort.

Aileen	Now let me go, if you will, and see her.
Proetus	No, I will. I am the one due, my love. Here comes Mother from the field, a sun flow'r in her basket.

(Exit Proetus and enter Echo)

Echo	There, there, Aileen, and here is a small thing I brought you from the gardens for your room.
Aileen	Oh, thank you, Echo, I treasure sunflow'rs for their color, their seed and oil, you know, and the conjuring lift they somehow weep to any body that will smile on them.
Echo	Oh, yes, and I know I'll be testing you with this incredible story, but truth hangs all over it. I was in Naissus some years back and, on my honor now, watched with both eyes wide and in the broad daylight a coyote seated before a sunflow'r trying to sway it with a smile. My heart on it! Poor thing, without the facial disc we have and that ponderous nose, he lacked control for it, but he tried. Where's daughter?
Aileen	In the house now, she and Proetus both.
Echo	Leaving you here?
	(Muted voices from the house)
Aileen	To enjoy you, Echo. It's the first time we have had together and already I am rich by one tale.
Echo	Would you like another, or to give one?

Aileen	It's my turn and I'll turn to honor it.
	My little story will have Socrates
	and an exotic dancer discussing
	her dance floor. Is it her floor to dance on
	or a couch that was used for eating on?
	She did a dance there; he reclined and ate.
	Socrates told her that idea came first,
	and the thing's idea was that of a couch.
	Since Athenians ate almost reclined,
	its obvious use was that for eating.
	No, cried the dancer; it was her dance floor.
	Use was everything; so who won that spat?

| Echo | Hard to tell, that one. |

Aileen	Yes indeed, Echo.
	I meant to say that questions oftentimes
	have value far beyond one good response.
	What we do is see eye to eye.

Echo	Heartfelt
	it is for you to say so. I feel it.
	I knew our first meeting that we were kin
	of the heart and mind and both delighted
	by it. But to tell the stale, lonely truth,
	I'm out of stories. They're fast out of mind,
	some gone with lightest wind. You heard the lone
	offering of my wit.

Aileen	One more likeness
	between us, Echo. I have no more, too.
	They are fun, but I would rather listen
	than tell one story.

(A cry from the house)

Who is that?!

Echo	My son!

(Both women stand as Proetus arrives at the doorway
with a knife in him.
Coming through the door, he settles onto the ground
in a Buddha's posture, looking to Aileen).

(Enter Dorthea)

Dorthea	There lies my man who would love two women!

He rode to the sunset for one he loved;
the other he turned his back on! Ay, ay;
nothing comes of uneven attentions!!
I gave him my only body, made home
to his comfort, ay, and oiled his bath.
She gave him what? Promises? No, not even!
She gave him the gift of language, fine thoughts,
a hand to hold, memory of a bed
warmed some forty years ago and as cold
now as memory claims! She denied me!
Received him! Well, then, let her take him now!
Ay, gods, let him go to her when he will;
he is nothing to me: a dried oak stump,
stone of curded blood. He would treasure me
to go hand in hand with him to the fields,
to the hedges where the rock buntings breed,
then to hear the wheatear's song and return
along banks of blood hibiscus. Would I?
I would be a fool not to, Proetus!
The blood hibiscus are for you alone,
Proetus!! Ay, for you! Rot where you lie,
then, not in her heart nor anywhere!

The End